Why Tomorrow?

First Edition   1983

ISBN 0-8351-1094-X

Published by the Foreign Languages Press
24 Baiwanzhuang Road, Beijing, China

Printed by the Foreign Languages Printing House
19 West Chegongzhuang Road, Beijing, China

Distributed by China Publications Centre (Guoji Shudian)
P.O. Box 399, Beijing, China

Printed in the People's Republic of China

Why Tomorrow?

Adapted by Li Shufen
Illustrations by Jiang Cheng'an

FOREIGN LANGUAGES PRESS   BEIJING

Look at all the wonderful trees in the forest. What a grand and beautiful place!

Many kinds of lovely flowers grew in this forest, too. Their fragrance attracted colourful butterflies and bees.

The sun was shining especially bright. It was a perfect day!

The animals of the forest all came out to dance. They were having a great time, when suddenly...

The weather changed. A fierce wind began to blow and it rained. The frogs, delighted, sat on the big lotus leaves and sang: "Croak, croak, croak!"

Squirrel jumped onto the trunk of a tree. He had made a hole there big enough for him to get in.

The hedgehog had a speckled house, just like a giant mushroom.

Only Monkey got wet in the rain because he had no house to go to. He just grabbed a lotus leaf and laughed. "Not a bad umbrella!" he said.

But just then a gust of wind blew the lotus leaf up, and Monkey with it.

Soon Monkey couldn't hold on any longer and he fell down. Luckily he lit on the branch of a tree and wasn't hurt.

He was so wet and uncomfortable that he jumped about but still found no place to get out of the rain. "Tomorrow I'll build a house," he said to himself, "a new house with windows and curving roof".

The rain stopped. Monkey quickly gathered branches and palm leaves. Was he really going to build himself a house?...

It was such a fine day! Better play in such fine weather and put off building the house till tomorrow.

Monkey played and played till it was getting dark and he was tired out.

The next day dawned bright and sunny.

Squirrel got up early and gathered nuts for breakfast.

Woodpecker started work first thing in the morning — pecking out insect pests from a big tree.

What about Monkey that fine morning?

He was drawing a plan for his house. He drew one but thought it was too small. So he drew a bigger one.

Not bad! The house was high off the ground and had good wide eaves.

But Squirrel was worried. "When can you finish building a house as big as that?" Monkey replied: "Why, tomorrow. I'll finish it by tomorrow."

Monkey said happily to Squirrel: "Tomorrow I'll have a new house and invite you all to my housewarming!"

In Monkey's mind he already had a new house, so he went to invite his guests. First he went to see Big Elephant.

Yes, and there was Sister Oriole. She was so excited to hear the news that she shouted for joy: "Monkey's building a new house and inviting us to his housewarming tomorrow!"

Woodpecker, Owl, Peacock and a lot of others heard Oriole and began shouting happily: "We'll all be at Monkey's housewarming tomorrow!"

Monkey hurried down to the lake to invite the frogs to visit him tomorrow in his new house. The frogs accepted with pleasure, saying "Croak, croak, croak!"

Monkey ran about all day inviting this one and that one, and the whole day was gone.

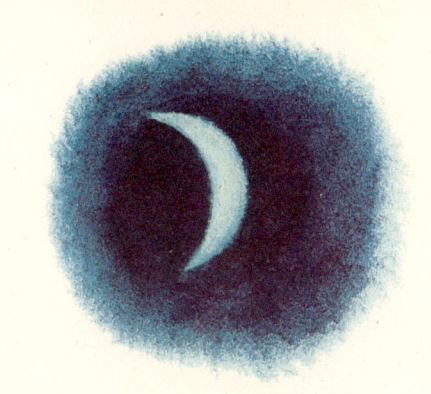

Monkey was so tired at the end of the day that he lay down on a palm leaf, looked up at the moon and said to himself: "It's too late today. I'd better build my house tomorrow." He fell asleep at once and had a dream.

In his dream Monkey saw his new house going up. How high its roof was, how wide its eaves, and how red its pillars....

Flowers bloomed, birds sang, making a big, beautiful garden around his new house.

Flower petals of lovely colours floated in the air. Monkey felt on top of the world. What a magnificent house! Everyone would be green with envy!

It was time for the guests to arrive, and they came singing and dancing. Crane and Fox did a demonstration dance.

Peacock spread his gorgeous tail in delight.

Two frogs then performed their "invitation dance".

Big Elephant did a solo dance that made everyone laugh.

The squirrels presented a graceful "ring dance".

Monkey, still in his dream, climbed onto the roof of his dream house and hung a colourful lantern on it.

Monkey's friends were having a wonderful time. They threw him into the air, shouting: "One, two!" Then they counted, "One, two!" again and threw him up again.

What a sweet dream Monkey was having!

But the night was over. The giraffe, with Woodpecker, the frogs and Turtle on her back, was making her way to where Monkey lay sleeping.

Big Elephant, with Badger, Fox and Hedgehog on his back, was going to Monkey's new house, too.

Peacock and the orioles were also strutting and flying to Monkey's place.

The whole Rabbit family, Squirrel and Bear Cub were coming too.

Still dreaming, Monkey felt his house shaking. What's happened? Oh, that giraffe! He was shaking Monkey's "house".

Squirrel called gently: "Hello, wake up! Everybody's here. Where's your new house?"

Monkey awoke from his dream. He opened his eyes and finally managed to say: "But didn't I tell you to come tomorrow? My new house will be ready tomorrow!"

"Isn't today 'yesterday's 'tomorrow'? Where will you go if it rains today?" asked his friends.

It so happened that at mention of the word "rain" it started to rain, and thunder, and lightning.

With no place to get out of the rain, everybody hurried back home. Only Monkey scurried about, but he still got awfully wet.

Who was to blame but himself? Monkey was always saying: "I'll do that tomorrow." But tomorrow never came and in the end he did nothing but play, and sleep, and dream. Maybe the rain helped Monkey to get rid of his bad habit of putting things off till "tomorrow".

Anyway, what Monkey did was to get busy before the rain stopped building himself a house. Now Monkey had a new house.

等 明 天

李树芬　改编
姜成安　绘画

*

外文出版社出版
(中国北京百万庄路24号)
外文印刷厂印刷
中国国际书店发行
(北京399信箱)
1983年（横16开）第一版
编号：（英）8050—2309
00280　（精）
00180　（平）
88—E—231